AF583159

One night, Taylor was lying in bed, his head filled with the memories of love that he sees only when he closes his eyes. He remembers giving great, big bear hugs to his Great Grandpa, playing rocks with his Granddad, and throwing the ball with his Rexy Boy.

When his mom comes to sing him to sleep that night, he asks her, with tears in his eyes, "Mommy, I am so sad they are gone, who will fix my heart?" As his mom holds him in her arms, she tells him the story of the "Fixers".

We all have Fixers inside of us and, when we feel safe enough to let them, they can take us on a journey where we will learn to do hard things. At the end of your journey, you will find a home was built for your heart; to keep it safe.

The first step on your journey will be with Sadness. It will look messy or feel bad and you might cry. Do you remember the morning you woke up and snuggled with mom, dad and brother and we told you that Rex was gone?

Remember how we all stayed snuggled together and cried for a long time. Sometimes we feel safest starting our journey with Sadness when we stay close to people who love us.

Sadness will tear down the old home

around your heart that kept it safe.

As you grow up, you will rebuild your heart's home many times. You can't build a new home to make room for growing up until you have finished your journey with Sadness. It will make sure the foundation of your heart's new home is strong enough to hold up the rest.

MOVERS
CAMP
Dear Mum + Dad, I miss you.
BASKETBALL TEAM ROSTER
RIP

Memories will be with you for the next part of your journey. You will find yourself surrounded with Memories that have helped you grow, even memories of the people and pets you can't talk to or hug anymore. Some Memories might be happy, others might be sad, and still more might be angry or scary.

But it's important to let them work together because all those Memories are important.

Do you remember going to Granddad's house and making him laugh with your silly faces?

Or how Great Grandpa would say "Hey there big guy, how about a bear hug?" every time he saw you?

Those are Memories we can keep in our hearts forever. Those Memories will live in the walls of your heart's home, and they are strong enough to hold up your roof.

You might start to feel Strength, Hope, and Joy. When this starts, Joy has started leading your journey. Joy does not rush and will give all the other Fixers time for their journey and to build your parts of the heart's home.

You will know Joy is there when you hear a certain song, or when a dragonfly stops by for a visit, or when you see an elk running through the trees or when you throw a stick into a lake.

These everyday things have been turned into magic by Joy. Joy brings all the parts of your heart's home together and will keep out the leaks with Strength and Hope.

STRENGTH
Hope
Joy

There is one more Fixer, and this one always surrounds you. It walks with you through your journey. With it you are never alone, even when you are by yourself. It is Love. Love comes from all the people around you, even those you can't see anymore.

Love is there for you when Sadness hurts, when Memories make you laugh or cry, and when Joy is ready to be shared. Love is always there to walk you home.

Every part of your journey is important and at times you will feel Sadness all over again, or Memories will take over your mind. I promise you can always come to me so that we can take care of those feelings and keep your heart's home strong.

Take your time through your journey of building your heart's home because each step you take is important. No step is done alone. When the Fixers are allowed, they will fix your heart, because you can do hard things.

www.ingramcontent.com/pod-product-compliance
Lightning Source LLC
LaVergne TN
LVHW071116160826
845679LV00004B/1102
* 9 7 8 1 7 7 7 5 8 8 7 0 0 *